ANIMAL INVADERS

AMANDA DOERING TOURVILLE

Rourke
Educational Media

rourkeeducationalmedia.com

www.rourkeeducationalmedia.com

Photo Credits: Cover: Clockwise from top left: David P. Lewis/Shutterstock Images, iStockphoto, Photographic Australia/Shutterstock Images, Hans Van Camp/Shutterstock Images, Vladimir Chernyandskiy. Interior: Photographic Australia/Shutterstock Images; 1, 32; Jeffrey Stone/ Shutterstock Images; 4; Stephen Strathdee/iStockphoto; 5; Felix Mizioznikov/Shutterstock Images; 6; Natural Resource Conservation Service; 7; Richard Cano/iStockphoto; 8 (top); Seleznev Valery/ Shutterstock Images; 8 (bottom); AZPworldwide/Shutterstock Images; 9; Andrea Gingerich/ iStockphoto; 10; Al Mueller/Shutterstock Images; 11; Steffen Foerster Photographer/Shutterstock Images; 12; Thomas Barrat/Shutterstock Images; 13; Tom C. Amon/Shutterstock Images; 14 (top); Shutterstock Images; 14 (bottom), 20, 31, 45; Matt Niebuhr/Shutterstock Images; 15; Martin Maun/Shutterstock Images; 16; Nico Smit/iStockphoto; 17 (top; Prill Mediendesign & Fotografie/ iStockphoto; 17 (middle); Tim Abbott/iStockphoto; 17 (bottom); Brett Hillyard/iStockphoto; 18 (top); Mau Horng/Shutterstock Images; 18 (bottom); iStockphoto; 19, 24, 28 (top), 41; Red Line Editorial, Inc.; 21 (top), 33 (top); Eric Isselée/iStockphoto; 21 (bottom); Bruce MacQueen/iStockphoto; 22; Jens Ottoson/Shutterstock Images; 23; Dorling Kindersley; 25; Vladimir Chernyandskiy/iStockphoto; 26; Laurie L. Snidow/iStockphoto; 27 (top); Photograph courtesy of the U.S. Geological Survey; 27 (second from top); Scott Bauer/United States Department of Agriculture; 27 (second from bottom), 28 (bottom); Peggy Greb/United States Department of Agriculture; 27 (bottom); Paul Roux/ iStockphoto; 29; Michael Pettigrew/Shutterstock Images; 30; David P. Lewis/Shutterstock Images; 33 (bottom); NatalieJean/Shutterstock Images; 34; Eugene Gordin/Shutterstock Images; 35; Sherwin McGehee/iStockphoto; 36; Vassiliy Vishnevskiy/iStockphoto; 37 (top); Rui Saraiva/iStockphoto; 37 (bottom); Holger W./Shutterstock Images; 38; Damian Herde/Shutterstock Images; 39; Marek Mnich/iStockphoto; 40; Jamie Wilson/iStockphoto; 42 (top); Iain Sarjeant/iStockphoto; 42 (bottom); Douglas Allen/iStockphoto; 43; Tim Osborne/iStockphoto; 44

Editor: Amy Van Zee

Cover and page design: Kazuko Collins

Content Consultant: Martha Groom, Professor of Conservation Biology, University of Washington

Library of Congress Cataloging-in-Publication Data
Tourville, Amanda Doering, 1980-
 Animal invaders / Amanda Doering Tourville.
    p. cm. -- (Let's explore science)
 Includes bibliographical references and index.
 ISBN 978-1-61590-319-1 (hard cover)(alk. paper)
 ISBN 978-1-61590-558-4 (soft cover)
 1. Introduced animals--United States--Juvenile literature. 2. Habitat conservation--United States--Juvenile literature. I. Title.
 QL86.T68 2011
 591.6'2--dc22
                                              2010009906

Rourke Educational Media
Printed in the United States of America,
North Mankato, Minnesota

rourkeeducationalmedia.com

customerservice@rourkeeducationalmedia.com • PO Box 643328 Vero Beach, Florida 32964

Table of Contents

What Are Animal Invaders? 4

Where Do They Come From and
How Do They Get Here? 18

What Harm Do Invasive Species Cause? 24

The Worst Offenders 32

Controlling Invasive Species 38

Glossary 46

Index 48

Chapter 1

WHAT ARE ANIMAL INVADERS?

Wooden crates from China arrive at a busy warehouse in the United States. Workers are so busy unpacking the materials that they do not notice a black beetle peeking out from one of the crates. The beetle scurries across the floor and underneath the warehouse door.

Invasive species can travel to new locations on cargo ships.

DID YOU KNOW?

Technology has made it easier for people to travel farther. People in the United States also consume many products that are imported from other countries. Increased travel and importation raise the risk of carrying an **invasive species** to a new location.

Sugar cane farmers in Hawaii have a problem with insects eating their crops. The farmers import the cane toad from South America to eat the insects. The toads grow very large and breed rapidly. They are poisonous to anything that tries to eat them. Now, the cane toads are the real pests.

These are examples of animal invaders. The animals are brought to a new environment. Sometimes they are brought accidentally and sometimes on purpose. These animals have invaded parts of the United States. They have caused problems in their new **habitats**. They have become invasive species.

Some invasive species can cling to the undersides of boats and be brought to new bodies of water.

HABITAT HOMES: NATIVES VS. INVADERS

A habitat is the natural environment where an animal lives. The habitat provides everything that the animal needs to survive. This includes food, water, and shelter. Most animals adapt to the habitat in which they live. This means they have the characteristics they need to survive there. For example, camels have long eyelashes to protect their eyes from the blowing dirt and sand in the deserts where they live. Because most animals are specifically adapted to their habitats, they are not usually able to survive in a completely different environment.

Native animals are animals that existed in their habitats before the arrival of humans. **Nonnative animals** are animals that have been brought to a new location.

Invasive species are those nonnative species that cause harm to other species in the **ecosystem** where they have been introduced. Usually, nonnative animals are transferred through human activity. The introduction of these new animals can often cause serious problems. When problems arise, the animal becomes an invasive species.

Nonnative species usually only survive if a new location is a similar habitat to the one the animal came from. An animal that is used to living in a forest with lots of water and trees would die in a dry desert.

Cattle are nonnative animals to North America. They provide humans with milk, meat, and hide.

Not all nonnative animals are invasive. Many nonnative species are good. For example, the **livestock** raised in the United States, such as cows, pigs, and chickens, are not native to North America. European settlers brought these animals to be raised for food. Europeans also brought honeybees. Bees pollinate flowers and many crops.

Only about 10 to 15 percent of newly introduced animals **establish** themselves and breed in their new habitats. The rest die. Fewer than one percent of nonnative animals will create problems in their new environments.

Bees produce products such as honey and beeswax that are helpful to humans.

But these invasive species can cause huge damage. Invasive animals cause habitat destruction. They sometimes threaten and even cause **extinction** of native plants and animals. They also can cause billions of dollars in damage. Animal invaders can even cause harm to humans through bites and diseases.

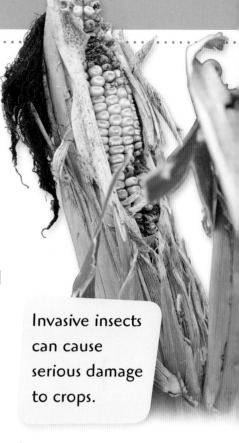

Invasive insects can cause serious damage to crops.

Each type of environment on Earth is distinguished by climate and the species that live there. Five of the most common environments are aquatic, grassland, tundra, forest, and desert.

DID YOU KNOW?

What makes a species invasive? Here are some common traits among invasive animal species:
- They are nonnative.
- They are capable of doing harm to native habitats, the economy, or public health.
- They have few natural predators in their new habitats.
- They reproduce at high rates.
- They are able to compete with native species for resources such as food and space.
- They are able to **thrive** in different locations.

AQUATIC HABITATS

Aquatic environments can be seawater or freshwater. Seawater habitats have a high amount of salt. Oceans are vast seawater habitats. They are full of life, from the smallest one-celled animals to the largest whales. Oceans are home to fish such as sharks and stingrays and mammals such as dolphins, whales, manatees, and seals. Many species of turtles, snakes, crabs, shrimp, lobsters, jellyfish, octopuses, and worms also live in the ocean.

Fish, coral, and sea anemones live together in ocean habitats.

Freshwater environments include ponds, lakes, streams, rivers, and wetlands. Wetlands and other freshwater habitats are home to many animals, including fish. Other animals that live in freshwater habitats include beavers, otters, frogs, turtles, alligators, and crocodiles. Many birds such as ducks, cranes, and storks nest near wetlands.

Aquatic invaders can spread easily. Some attach to boats and are moved from one body of water to another. Others are introduced on purpose. Aquatic invaders in the United States include nutria and zebra **mussels**.

Cranes build nests in wetlands and other shallow waters.

Some African savannas are very dry. Animals may have a hard time finding enough water.

GRASSLANDS

Grasslands occur from hot to cold climates, ranging from savanna to prairie. Grasslands primarily have grasses and few or no trees. North American prairies are home to bison, deer, coyotes, jackrabbits, snakes, mice, and prairie dogs. Birds also soar above prairies looking for mice and other rodents.

Cattle often graze on grasslands, but they are not native to the United States. **Feral** cattle can form wild herds and damage prairies by trampling vegetation. In Hawaii, feral cattle have prevented the growth of some native plants.

TUNDRA

Unlike savannas and prairies, the tundra is very cold. Temperatures can reach –70 degrees Fahrenheit (–55 degrees Celsius). The land is usually covered in snow or ice and the deep soil is permanently frozen. The northern tundra is home to caribou, wolves, and several types of birds.

Some animals have moved into the northern tundra from southern habitats. These animals threaten native animal species. For example, the red fox competes with the native arctic fox for food and resources.

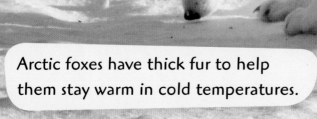

Arctic foxes have thick fur to help them stay warm in cold temperatures.

FORESTS

Forest environments also span a wide range of climates. Tropical rainforests are warm throughout the year, and they receive a lot of rain. Although tropical forests cover only six percent of the Earth's surface, they are home to an enormous number of plants and animals. Tropical forests are home to jaguars, monkeys, colorful birds, frogs, snakes, butterflies, and thousands of other species.

Tropical frogs come in many bright colors.

Some tropical rainforests have more than 250 different types of trees. Almost half of the plant species in the world grow in tropical rainforests.

Temperate forests are much cooler than tropical forests. Although they usually receive less rain than tropical forests, temperate forests receive enough rainfall to support many trees. These forest habitats are home to animals such as deer, bears, foxes, wolves, rabbits, squirrels, and many birds and insects.

Nonnative animals such as wild pigs and goats can do damage to forest habitats. They dig up the earth and destroy vegetation. The red deer was introduced to North and South American countries. These deer interfere with native plant growth and compete with other native animals for food and space.

In many forests winters can be very cold. Some forest animals hibernate during the cold winter months.

DESERTS

Desert habitats are also found on every continent and are very dry. They receive less than ten inches (25.4 centimeters) of moisture each year. Temperatures in the Sahara Desert in Africa can reach up to 120 degrees Fahrenheit (50 degrees Celsius) during a summer day. Deserts are not always hot. The Sahara is cool in the winter and at night.

Desert animals are equipped to handle life without much water. Animals in the desert include foxes, lizards, snakes, and many types of spiders and scorpions. The red imported fire ant is one type of invasive species that affects desert habitats. These ants sting and inject venom into their enemies. Many humans are stung each year.

Because deserts receive very little rainfall, few plants and animals are able to survive in desert habitats.

Scorpion

Lizard

Fox

Chapter 2

WHERE DO THEY COME FROM AND HOW DO THEY GET HERE?

Invasive species come from all over the world. They have inhabited almost every part of North America. These animal invaders are transferred by natural or human-induced pathways.

Animals sometimes get to distant habitats by natural pathways. Ocean currents, wind currents, and hitchhiking on other animals are some ways that species are introduced to new locations.

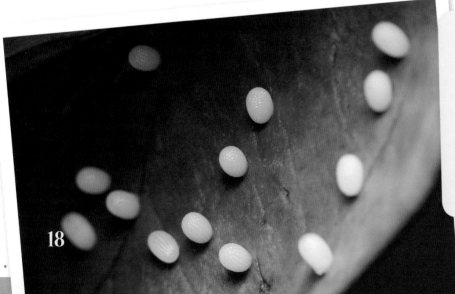

Tiny insect eggs attach to leaves and can be brought to new places by animals or the wind.

DID YOU KNOW?

The European starling is a black bird with light spots. From 1890 to 1891, 100 of these birds were released in Central Park in New York City. A man who enjoyed William Shakespeare's plays wanted to bring every bird mentioned in Shakespeare's works to the United States. The population of the starling has now reached 200 million birds. They can be found all over North America. Starlings gather in large flocks. They have become major pests in some southern states.

Human-induced pathways are the most common source of animal invasion. Human-induced pathways are caused by activities such as international shipping, travel, the pet trade, farming methods, and food markets. As international human activities increase, so do the opportunities for potentially invasive species to spread to new habitats across the world. Human-induced pathways can either be **intentional** or **unintentional**.

Nutria can weigh 20 pounds (9 kilograms).

Animals are often brought into new locations intentionally for food, as pets, or to fight other invasive species. The nutria is a large rodent that was brought to Louisiana from South America in the 1930s. People hoped to raise them for their fur. Once they were released into the wild they invaded swamps and wetlands.

Many small invasive animals, such as insects, are introduced by accident. These species are carried on cargo ships, in shipping crates, or in the water or soil taken on by ships. Many also traveled on timber or plants.

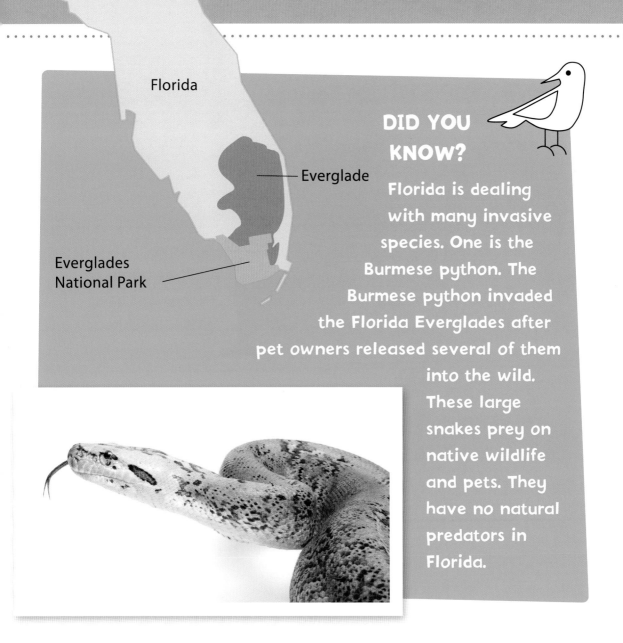

Florida

Everglade

Everglades
National Park

DID YOU KNOW?

Florida is dealing with many invasive species. One is the Burmese python. The Burmese python invaded the Florida Everglades after pet owners released several of them into the wild. These large snakes prey on native wildlife and pets. They have no natural predators in Florida.

But animal invaders do not always come from faraway places. Sometimes an animal that is native to one part of the country will spread to other parts of the same country. Often this new location is separated from the native location by a large barrier, such as a mountain range.

Without predators, bullfrog populations in the West have grown quickly.

For example, the bullfrog is native to the eastern and central parts of the United States but was never found west of the Rocky Mountains. In the late 1800s, bullfrogs were brought to California for food. At the time, many people enjoyed eating frog legs. But some frogs were released into the wild.

In the eastern and central United States, bullfrogs are not a problem. Predators there eat bullfrogs and their eggs. But in the West, bullfrogs have few predators. Their numbers quickly grew out of control. Bullfrogs prey on native western animals and have nearly wiped out a native species of frog, the Chiricahua leopard frog, in Arizona.

Even cats and dogs can become invasive animals. They are not native to the United States. Sometimes people cannot take care of their pets. They think that they are being kind by leaving the animals in the wild. Sometimes these animals die. But sometimes they survive and become wild animals that can harm other species or spread disease.

Animals that were once pets but become wild are called feral animals. Feral cats prey on wild birds. They can hurt or kill pet cats that are let outside. Feral dogs eat pets and livestock such as chickens. They will sometimes even attack humans.

Some experts estimate that there are more than 70 million feral cats living in the United States.

Chapter 3

WHAT HARM DO INVASIVE SPECIES CAUSE?

Invasive species compete with and even eat native animals. Invasive species can also bring diseases to their new habitats, killing native plants and animals. Some animal invaders destroy habitats. Others damage crops. This can cost millions of dollars. Some native species can even harm humans.

Coral reefs are rich in plant and animal species.

Invasive species are a threat to **biodiversity**. Biodiversity encompasses the diversity of living forms on Earth, including the variety of genetic types, species, and ecosystems. Areas with a high level of biodiversity may be better able to withstand **infestation** of nonnative species.

Invasive species can cause disruptions in the **food chain**. All ecosystems have multiple food chains, in which certain animals eat other animals, which in turn eat other organisms or plants.

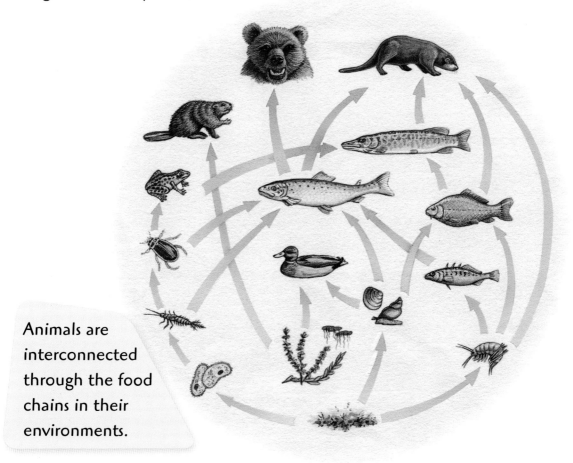

Animals are interconnected through the food chains in their environments.

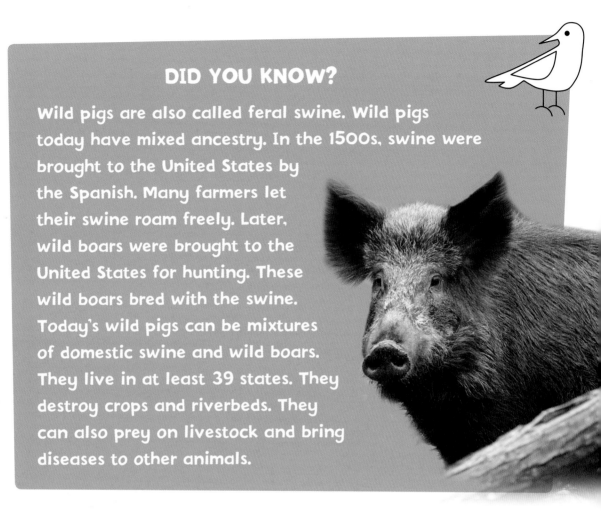

DID YOU KNOW?

Wild pigs are also called feral swine. Wild pigs today have mixed ancestry. In the 1500s, swine were brought to the United States by the Spanish. Many farmers let their swine roam freely. Later, wild boars were brought to the United States for hunting. These wild boars bred with the swine. Today's wild pigs can be mixtures of domestic swine and wild boars. They live in at least 39 states. They destroy crops and riverbeds. They can also prey on livestock and bring diseases to other animals.

When an invasive species comes to a new environment, the species competes with native animals for food, space, and other resources. If the competition becomes fierce enough, the invasive animal can reduce population sizes and even cause extinction of native species. This can affect other species in the food chain. The competition from invasive species can cause problems all the way through the food chain.

	Invasive Animal	Effect on Native Plant and Animal Life	Affected Region
	Feral pigs	Feral pigs root up native plants and damage the habitat for other animals.	Many parts of the United States including Texas, California, and the South
	New Zealand mud snails	The New Zealand mud snail out-competes native snails for resources. Its introduction has led to decreases in populations of native snails and fish.	Snake River in Idaho, the Great Lakes
	European gypsy moth caterpillars	The European gypsy moth caterpillar weakens and kills trees by eating their leaves. Birds and other species that lived in these trees are forced to find new habitats.	Many parts of the United States, especially the Northeast
	Glassy-winged sharpshooter	The glassy-winged sharpshooter passes bacteria to grape plants. These bacteria kill the plant by blocking its water and nutrient systems.	California

Mediterranean fruit fly

Insects cause the most problems for crops in the United States. The Mediterranean fruit fly lays its eggs on developing fruit. The fruit becomes food for the new flies. This damages the fruit. Much of this fruit cannot be sold or has to be sold at cheaper prices.

The silverleaf whitefly feeds on the sap of plants and can introduce bacteria from plant to plant. The silverleaf whitefly has been known to attack more than 500 different plants, including tomato, cotton, and peanut plants.

Silverleaf whitefly

African honeybee

The African honeybee was brought to Brazil in 1956 to breed with European honeybees. People hoped that these hybrid insects would produce more honey. The Africanized honeybee spread from South America to the southern United States in the 1990s.

Africanized honeybees are not picky about where they nest. An old tire, a mailbox, or a shed makes a perfect hive for them. Humans can easily come into contact with these **aggressive** bees. They are very quick to protect their hives and will chase and sting humans and animals that invade their territories. These "killer bee" swarms have caused several human deaths.

The Asian tiger mosquito can carry the West Nile virus and can transfer the virus to humans. West Nile virus has been around since 1937, but the United States diagnosed its first case in 1999. Most healthy people who have the West Nile virus may feel sick for a few days. Most recover completely. For some elderly people, people who are already sick, or pregnant women, the virus can be harmful. Some people can experience permanent brain damage or even die. Invasive plants and animals also affect quality of life for many people.

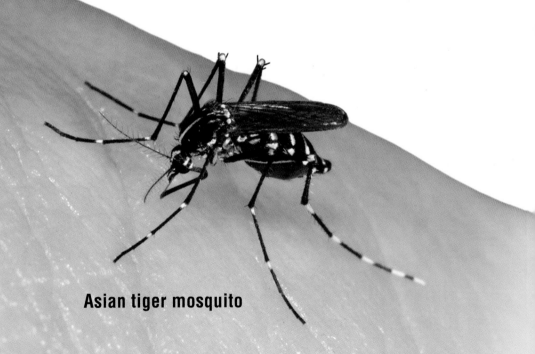

Asian tiger mosquito

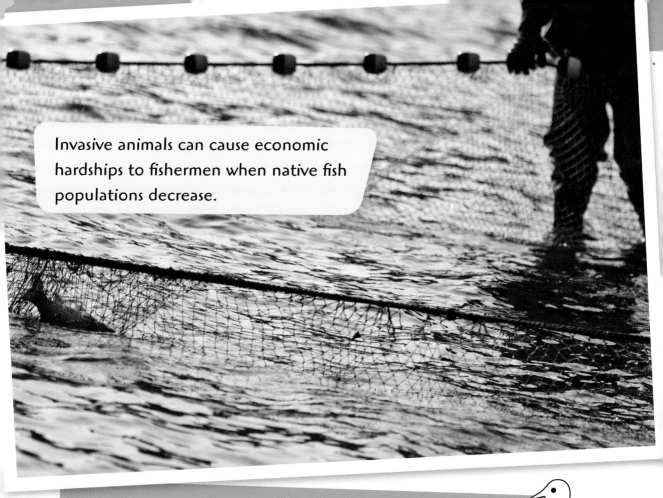

Invasive animals can cause economic hardships to fishermen when native fish populations decrease.

DID YOU KNOW?

Invasive species, which also include invasive plants, are estimated to cost 138 billion dollars in damages and losses every year. This estimate accounts for expenses such as lost crop production and lost revenues from decreased tourism and recreation.

People who enjoy outdoor activities such as hunting and fishing may be affected when native species decline. The loss of habitat can also negatively affect parks and nature preserves that many people enjoy.

THE WORST OFFENDERS

All invasive species cause damage. Some invasive species have seriously disrupted native habitats.

The brown tree snake is native to Australia and Indonesia. This snake was introduced to Guam, a U.S. territory, in the 1950s. It likely was brought with imported cargo. The brown tree snake has no natural predators on Guam. It has since eliminated several native species of birds and lizards, killed pets and livestock, and has even caused power outages by climbing electrical wires!

Brown tree snake

Lake Michigan

Lake Superior

Lake Huron

Lake Ontario

Lake Erie

The zebra mussel is a small freshwater mollusk. It is native to the Black and Caspian Seas. Zebra mussels

Mississippi River

were first noticed in the Great Lakes in the late 1980s. They have since spread to the Mississippi River and many smaller rivers. Large ships transferred them. These ships take on native water to sail and then release the water when they arrive at **port**.

Young zebra mussels are free-floating and can be spread by water currents. Adult zebra mussels attach themselves to boats, water intake pipes, crayfish, turtles, and other native animals. This interferes with the movement, reproduction, and feeding of the native species.

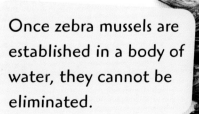

Once zebra mussels are established in a body of water, they cannot be eliminated.

The red imported fire ant is native to South America. It is now found throughout the southeastern United States. The ants were accidentally introduced from soil brought in ships. These ants can cause painful stings to humans, pets, and livestock. The sting leaves a blister that can become infected. These ants destroy trees and crops. Getting rid of red imported fire ants is hard because they look similar to native ants.

Red imported fire ants

Nutria

Nutria were
brought to Louisiana
to be raised for fur. When the fur market
declined in the 1940s, the animals were released into
the wild. The nutria can now be found throughout the
southeastern United States, where they have few natural
predators. They reproduce rapidly and tear up wetland
habitats to eat the roots of plants. Nutria also eat crops
such as sugarcane and corn. Nutria can also carry
diseases that can be spread to other animals and humans.

Emerald ash borer

The emerald ash borer is native to Asia. It is now found in 13 states in the United States. This insect probably made its way to the United States in wood crates and packing materials. The emerald ash borer infests ash trees, weakening and eventually killing the trees. Animals that depend on ash trees for food and shelter are negatively affected. The wood from ash trees is used in flooring and furniture, so the loss of trees has economic impacts as well.

Birds that live in ash trees may be displaced when emerald ash borers invade.

DID YOU KNOW?

The house mouse is common in the United States, but it can be found in many places throughout the world. The house mouse is thought to be native to Asia. It was brought to the Americas in the ships of early European explorers. The house mouse lives close to humans. House mice can breed quickly, and they often spread disease. They are capable of destroying crops too.

Chapter 5

CONTROLLING INVASIVE SPECIES

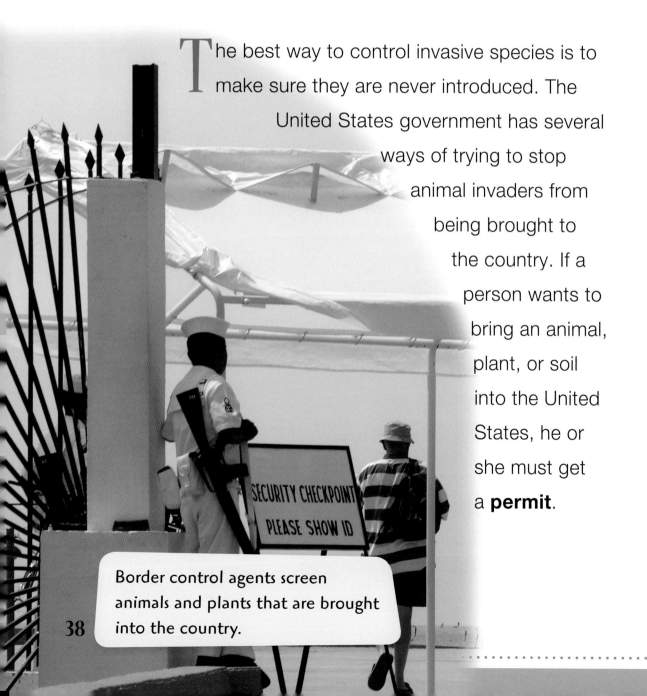

The best way to control invasive species is to make sure they are never introduced. The United States government has several ways of trying to stop animal invaders from being brought to the country. If a person wants to bring an animal, plant, or soil into the United States, he or she must get a **permit**.

Border control agents screen animals and plants that are brought into the country.

Animal and Plant Health Inspection Services gives out these permits. They help make sure the animal, plant, or soil is safe.

When a person passes over a border into the United States, he or she must go through an inspection. These are done to make sure that plants and animals are not brought into the country illegally. Government and environmental groups have educated international companies and trade partners about the possible risks of invasive species.

States such as Oregon have developed plans to get rid of feral swine populations.

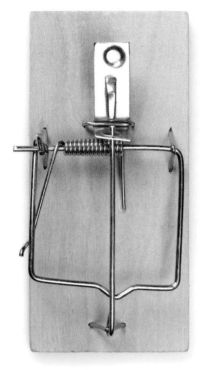

In some places, trapping has been an effective tool for controlling invasive species populations.

Once an invasive species is introduced, scientists, the government, organizations, and volunteer groups work to fight the spread of these harmful species. These invasive species can rarely be completely removed, but they can be controlled.

Mechanical controls include burning nests, hunting, trapping, or inserting barriers so that animals cannot get through. For example, nutria have been trapped in the southern United States. Mounds of red imported fire ants have been burned. Barriers have been created so that zebra mussels cannot attach themselves to water intake pipes.

Chemical controls are the application of chemicals to control invasive species populations. This can include pesticides and insecticides to get rid of pests. Some chemical controls are effective, but they can harm other species too. They can also harm humans. Chemicals can get on crops that humans eat.

Pesticides can kill problematic insects, but they sometimes hurt the environment.

Many groups teach the public about animal invaders. See if you can get involved!

Biological control involves introducing another species that can control the animal invader. Usually this is done by introducing a predator that will eat the invasive species. This method may be difficult to control. The newly introduced predator may prey on native animals, or it may become an invasive species itself.

Sometimes biological control is done with a parasite. A parasite gets its food by living on or near another organism. The parasite may make individuals of the invasive species sick, causing them to die or preventing them from reproducing.

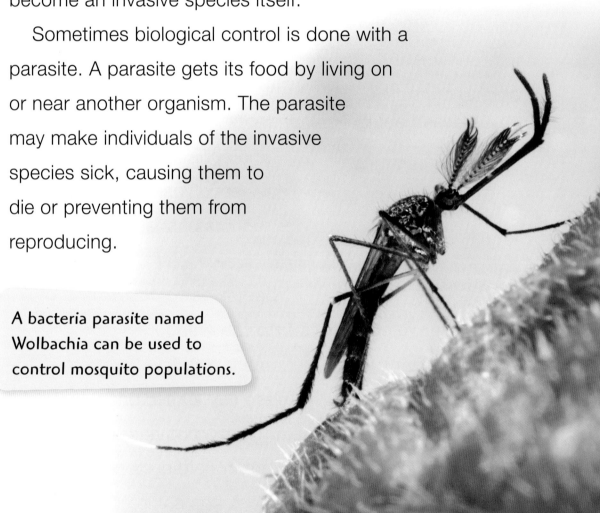

A bacteria parasite named Wolbachia can be used to control mosquito populations.

It is important to check and clean beneath boats before moving them to a new body of water.

There are many things that people can do to stop the introduction and spread of invasive species. These are steps you can take to keep native plant and animal species safe.

- **Never release pets into the wild.**
  Find your pet a new home instead.
- **If you fish, never release live bait into the wild.**
  You could be introducing a nonnative species into a new environment or spreading a disease to animals in that habitat.

- **If you boat, clean your boat thoroughly before taking it to a new lake or river.**

  Boat owners can accidentally transport invasive weeds, mussels, and fish to new bodies of water.

- **If you camp, use local firewood.**

  Forest pests can be transported to new habitats by campers who bring their own firewood from home.

- **Plant native species in your yard.**

  These plants can provide natural habitats for animals and keep diversity in the environment.

- **If you travel, never try to bring plants or animals home with you.**

  You could release a pest by accident.

Insects can live inside firewood and be transported along with it.

Glossary

aggressive (uh-GRESS-ive): to be eager to fight or confront

biodiversity (bye-oh-duh-VURS-it-ee): the number and variety of living things in an area

ecosystem (E-coh-sis-tum): a community of plants, animals, and the environment that function as a unit

establish (ess-TAB-lish): to introduce, grow, and multiply

extinction (ek-STINGK-shuhn): the act of not existing any longer

feral (FIR-uhl): wild

food chain (FOOD CHAYN): an order of animals and plants in which each feeds on the one below it

habitats (HAB-uh-tats): the places or environments where a plant or animal lives and grows

infestation (in-fess-TAY-shuhn): the spread of something in a negative manner

intentional (in-TEN-shuh-nuhl): done on purpose

invasive species (in-VAY-siv SPEE-sheez): a nonnative type of plant or animal that does damage in its new habitat

livestock (LIVE-stok): animals kept or raised for use and profit

mussels (MUHSS-uhlz): freshwater animals with shells

native animals (NAY-tiv AN-uh-muhlz): animals that existed in their habitats before the arrival of humans

nonnative animals (NON-nay-tiv AN-uh-muhlz): animals that have been brought to a new location

permit (PUR-mit): a written license to do something

port (PORT): a town or city where ships receive or send cargo

thrive (THRIVE): to prosper

unintentional (uhn-in-TEN-shuh-nuhl): done by accident

Index

Africanized honeybee   29

Asian tiger mosquito   30

biodiversity   24, 25

brown tree snake   32

bullfrog   22

Burmese python   21

cane toad   5

control   38, 40, 41, 43

damage   9, 12, 15, 19, 21, 22,
   23, 24, 26, 27, 28, 29, 30, 31,
   32, 33, 34, 35, 36, 37

emerald ash borer   36, 37

European gypsy moth
   caterpillars   27

European starling   19

feral animals   12, 23, 26, 27, 39

food chains   25, 26

glassy-winged sharpshooter   27

house mouse   37

Mediterranean fruit fly   28

New Zealand mud snail   27

nutria   11, 20, 35, 40

red imported fire ant   16, 34, 40

silverleaf whitefly   28

zebra mussels   11, 33, 40

Websites to Visit

http://animal.discovery.com/videos/animal-invaders/

www.glerl.noaa.gov/res/Programs/ncrais/kids.html

www.sciencenewsforkids.org/articles/20040512/Feature1.asp

www.sgnis.org/kids/

About the Author

Amanda Doering Tourville is the author of more than 50 books for children. She hopes that children will learn to love reading as much as she does. When she's not writing, Amanda enjoys reading, traveling, and hiking. She lives in Minnesota with her husband.